Designing Success
for Multilingual Learners
Second Edition

Designing Success for
Multilingual Learners:
*A Handbook of
Instructional Methods that Work*

Second Edition

Valentina Gonzalez

RootED Linguistics

This handbook is dedicated to all the teachers who give their time and love to students like I was and families like mine. The work you do is important and I hope you never lose sight of the impact you are making.
Thank you,

Introduction

This handbook was developed to support teachers of multilingual learners because I know what it's like to be a student who is acquiring English and I also know what it's like to a teacher with students who are learning English and learning new content. Both come with opportunities and challenges. This tiny handbook includes the most practical and powerful strategies for teaching multilingual learners from my experiences. The handbook was made to compliment the professional learning opportunities that I deliver in person and virtually but it can be used as a stand-alone guide to teachers and instructional coaches.

This is not a dense book that will take a lot of time to read. It is a handbook with selected, effective instructional techniques that can be used across grade levels and content areas. You will find that each of these strategies can also be implemented in whole groups or in small groups.

Instructional coaches and those who lead professional development for teachers can easily share these strategies in mini-PD sessions over time.

Designing Success for Multilingual Learners Second Edition

What's Inside

- Students ♥
- Developing a Complete Picture of MLs ⭐
- Core Beliefs
- Language Development ⭐
- Yearly Planning
- Content Teachers & Language Specialists ⭐
- ABC Brainstorming
- Newcomer Guide ⭐
- The Jigsaw Method ⭐
- Picture Word Induction Model ♥
- Wordless Picture Books
- Interactive Word Wall
- Sentence Patterning Chart
- Define, Describe, Sketch
- Paragraph/Writing Relay ⭐
- Accessibility ⭐
- Reading Interest Survey ⭐
- Classroom Look Fors
- Listening, Speaking, Reading, & Writing at Home ♥
- Notes

 ⭐ new   ♥ updated

STUDENTS

Name	date of birth	Place of birth	Language(s)

Designing Success for Multilingual Learners Second Edition

STUDENTS

Name	date of birth	Place of birth	Language(s)

8

 StUDents

Name	date of birth	Place of birth	Language(s)

Designing Success for Multilingual Learners Second Edition

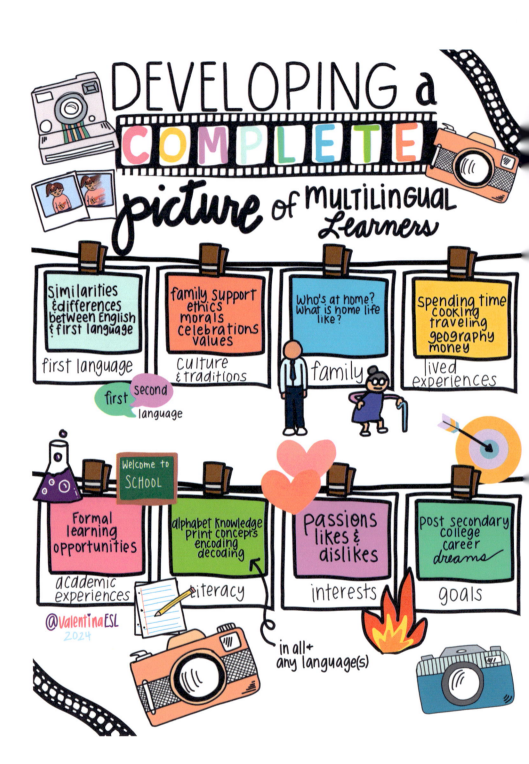

CORE BELIEFS

 Multilingual learners need daily opportunities to listen, speak, read, and write with their grade level peers.

 All language is valuable and should be used to acquire new language.

 Every classroom should be a space where all students feel welcome to participate.

 All teachers are responsible for language development and content learning.

Designing Success for Multilingual Learners Second Edition

CORE BELIEFS

What do you believe about serving multilingual learners? What anchors all that you do to serve multilingual learners?

Language is rooted to our identity. When we HIDe, SUPPRESS, or IGNORe this part of ourselves, we never truly flourish into the spectacular beauty we were designed to become.

- I believe...
- It's important that...
- When serving multilingual learners, we must remember...

So I will...

Designing Success for Multilingual Learners Second Edition

Language Development

Language production (grammar & vocabulary) is comparable to native speakers of the same age.

Advanced Flucency
5-7y

Communication to express ideas, feelings, and thoughts is increased and more accurate.

Intermediate Fluency
3-5y

Greater listening comprehension and increased production of simple sentences.

Speech Emergent
1-3y

Early Production
6m- 1y

Production of simple sentences and improved listening comprehension.

Preproduction
0-6m

Nonverbal responses such as pointing and nodding, sometimes called the silent period.

YEARLY plan

Year: _____

Aug	Sept	Oct
Nov	**Dec**	**Jan**
Feb	**Mar**	**Apr**
May	**June**	**July**

you are a linguistic genius.

Designing Success for Multilingual Learners Second Edition

CONTENT teachers and LANGUAGE SPECIALISTS

focus on grade level state standards

USE Language to teach content

focus on listening, speaking, reading, & writing

USE CONTENT to teach language

Share ideas
Plan together
Observe one another
Attend PD together
Co-create assessments

15

ABC BRAINSTORMING

with *MULTILINGUAL Learners*

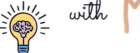

CREATIVE THINKING, ACCESSING PRIOR KNOWLEDGE & MORE

Accessing prior knowledge is an important element of instruction especially when serving multilingual learners. It doesn't have to take long, but when implemented it can stimulate thinking and help new learning stick too.

ABC Brainstorming is one way to access prior knowledge, and it can also be used as a culminating activity. ABC Brainstorming can be done in small collaborative groups or it can be done individually. I have found it most effective when introduced first individually for a few minutes and then in small collaborative groups.

This brainstorming technique is a structured method that provides each learner with an avenue for creative thinking. The organizer helps to methodically focus thinking while also allowing for individual exploration of ideas. It cultivates diversity in responses based on students' personal experiences and background knowledge. The student-centered approach affirms and validates learners' funds of knowledge.

There are several different formats for ABC Brainstorming. The most common includes 26 boxes, and another has nine boxes with roughly 3 letters in each box.

Designing Success for Multilingual Learners Second Edition

ABC BRAINSTORMING with MULTILINGUAL Learners

CREATIVE THINKING, ACCESSING PRIOR KNOWLEDGE & MORE

STEP-BY-STEP

1. Before a unit of study, decide which format of the ABC brainstorming best fits your student's needs. Print a copy for each student or prepare to share it with them digitally.
2. Share the ABC brainstorming organizer with students and have them brainstorm words and phrases related to the topic. Ask them to work independently for a given time.
3. Then put students in groups of four to collaborate on the ABC brainstorming organizer. Give them a given time to try to fill in all of the boxes together.
4. Under a document camera or on a SMARTboard, scribe the words that students dictate for each box.

17

ABC BRAINSTORMING with MULTILINGUAL Learners

CREATIVE THINKING, ACCESSING PRIOR KNOWLEDGE & MORE

As students work together and as a class to generate words, they continue to dig deeper into the concepts and learn new vocabulary from their peers. The versatility of the ABC brainstorming method is one of the reasons I find it practical. It can be used at the beginning and end of a unit or lesson with whole groups or small groups.

In some instances, multilingual learners will add words in languages other than English. I've also seen students include sketches or visuals in their brainstorming. All are valid and welcomed responses.

Overall, ABC brainstorming serves as a practical and engaging language practice activity that supports vocabulary expansion, grammar application, and creative expression for English learners. It can be integrated into language learning curricula to provide a structured and enjoyable way for learners to develop their language skills.

Designing Success for Multilingual Learners Second Edition

MULTILINGUAL Learners ABC BRAINSTORMING

A	B	C	D	E
F	G	H	I	J
K	L	M	N	O
P	Q	R	S	T
U	V	W	X	YZ

Designing Success for Multilingual Learners Second Edition

MULTILINGUAL Learners ABC BRAINSTORMING

ABC	**DEF**	**GHI**
JKL	**MNO**	**PQR**
STU	**VWX**	**YZ**

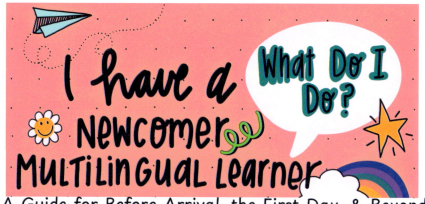

A Guide for Before Arrival, the First Day, & Beyond

BEFORE ARRIVAL

- ☐ Learn as much as you can about the new student.
- ☐ Pick the best seating arrangement for them.
- ☐ Get a name plate ready but don't write a name on it.
- ☐ Gather the necessary text books and tablets.
- ☐ Secure a translation dictionary, technology, etc.
- ☐ Collect a few school-related items like a t-shirt or folder to give to the new student as a welcome gift.

THE FIRST DAY OF ARRIVAL

- ☐ SMILE.
- ☐ Find out what the student prefers to be called. Learn to pronounce it.
- ☐ Reflect on the environment. Is it welcoming?
- ☐ Show the student around. Introduce them to teachers and staff.
- ☐ Key an eye on placement, seating, and resources. What else might the student need?

Designing Success for Multilingual Learners Second Edition

Things to keep in mind

Language acquisition strategies benefit ALL learners.
Language acquisition takes time. Be patient.
Keep the content and amplify the language.

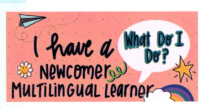

A Guide for Before Arrival, the First Day, & Beyond

THE FIRST WEEK & BEYOND

- ☐ Sit next to the new student. Confer with them.
- ☐ Learn a few words in their language.
- ☐ Label the room in English and in their language too.
- ☐ Encourage choral and echo reading providing lots of opportunities to hear and practice English.
- ☐ Provide frequent opportunities for peer and group interaction.
- ☐ Respect the silent period and language development. Even in silence, thinking is happening.
- ☐ Include all stakeholders. Collaboration for this student's success is a must.

notes

Designing Success for Multilingual Learners Second Edition

THE JIGSAW METHOD

The Jigsaw Method can be used with any age of students in all content areas.

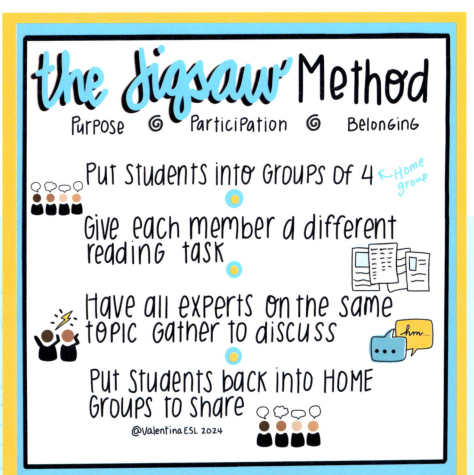

Designing Success for Multilingual Learners Second Edition

THE JIGSAW METHOD

The Jigsaw Method can be used with any age of students in all content areas.

Step-By-Step

1. Put students into mixed-level groups of about four. The levels can be based on skill, language, or concept knowledge. This group is the HOME group.
2. Take a reading passage, math problem, or concept and divide it into sections to distribute to each member of the HOME group. If there are four members, divide it into 4.
3. Give students time to become "experts" by reading, watching videos, looking at pictures, etc.
4. Gather all the experts on the same topic to discuss what they learned. (See *Options.)
5. Reconvene students into their HOME group.
6. Have each HOME group member share their findings and teach peers about the topic they were assigned. (See **Options for more.)

At A Glance

Opposed to teacher lecturing, the Jigsaw Method is an instructional technique that empowers, engages, and centers learners. It creates an atmosphere that encourages peer interaction and student participation.

THE JIGSAW METHOD

Extensions & Modifications

- *Some groups may benefit from structures like sentence stems. For example, "One thing I learned is that…" or "An important fact about…" "The most significant thing is…"

- **Provide group members with a graphic organizer or note-taking sheet to document their findings and what they learn from their peers.

- Students can be asked to become experts on an object or a visual such as something from their home.

Benefits

- Fosters a sense of purpose.
- Lowers the affective filter.
- Allows for participation with peers.
- Provides an opportunity to practice using academic language.
- Builds community.

Designing Success for Multilingual Learners Second Edition

PICTURE WORD INDUCTIVE MODEL (PWIM)

This teaching and learning method leverages students' background knowledge while building vocabulary and concepts.

(Calhoun, 1999 adapted by Valentina Gonzalez)

PICTURE word inductive model

lower the affective filter strengthen vocabulary participate with peers

adapted from the work of Emily Calhoun, 1998

 1 Select an image & present it to the class

 2 Have students brainstorm words & phrases independently

3 Have students share their lists with a partner

4 Label the image as a class

 5 Chorally read the labels

 6 Create sentences & paragraphs

practice academic vocabulary listen speak read write access background knowledge

PICTURE WORD INDUCTIVE MODEL (PWIM)

Step-By-Step

1. Select a picture related to the concept and present it for all students to see.
2. Introduce the picture and title it.
3. Have students brainstorm what they see.
4. Label the image as students share what they see.
5. Lead the class in chorally reading all the words that have been labeled.
6. Guide students in creating verbal sentences using sentence stems and the labeled picture as a word bank. Model and then have students turn to a partner and try.
7. Give students time to practice writing sentences using the sentence stems and the labeled picture as scaffolds.
8. Pair students up and have them read their sentences to one another.

27

PICTURE WORD INDUCTIVE MODEL (PWIM)

At A Glance

The Picture Word Inductive Model is a structured, yet student-centered approach to learning that helps students develop reading, writing, listening, and speaking skills. It is beneficial for multilingual learners at beginner levels of English proficiency as well as students who are learning new concepts and academic vocabulary. PWIM works by engaging students in active learning, peer collaboration, and the use of scaffolds.

Designing Success for Multilingual Learners Second Edition

PICTURE WORD INDUCTIVE MODEL (PWIM)

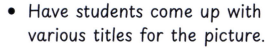

Extensions & Modifications

- Have students come up with various titles for the picture.
- Label by parts of speech using a different color marker to label for each.
- Collect a class bank of questions related to the visual.
- Create a shared or interactive writing (narrative or expository).
- Build a list of facts and opinions.

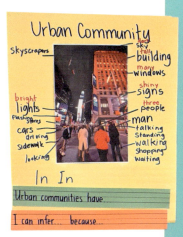

Benefits

- Strengthens vocabulary.
- Lowers the affective filter.
- Allows for participation with peers.
- Provides an opportunity to practice academic vocabulary and language.
- Yields access to background knowledge.
- Offers opportunities to recognize cognates.

WORDLESS PICTURE BOOKS

Picture books without words allow students to create their own language for each page, think critically about ideas, and engage in deep inference to develop a plot and theme while building language skills.

Using WORDLESS Picture Books with Multilingual Learners

- ✓ accessible in any language
- ✓ more easily processed
- ✓ pathways for oral & written storytelling
- ✓ free for interpretation
- ✓ ways to listen, speak, read, write, & think

WORDLESS PICTURE BOOKS

Step-By-Step

1. Select a wordless picture book and model "reading" it to the class.
2. Point to elements in the pictures as you "read" along.
3. Talk aloud the process of selecting the words you chose. "In this picture, the character's shoulders are low like this and look at his eyebrows. They are dropping down. He looks worried and sad. I'm going to add that here in the story."
4. When students are ready, ask them to turn and "read" a page to their partner.
5. After finishing the book, make it available for students to "read" independently or with a buddy.

At A Glance

Wordless picture books are often used with young learners and early elementary students. They are also beneficial for developing oral language skills in older multilingual learners. Wordless picture books are well-suited for oral and written storytelling. A key feature of wordless picture books is the power of sharing a story and interpreting visuals from multiple perspectives. Readers have the freedom to interpret the visuals through their own eyes, thoughts, and experiences, creating a culturally responsive practice.

31

WORDLESS PICTURE BOOKS

Extensions & Modifications

- As you "read" the book with the class, model a write-aloud of the text.
- Have students create their own wordless picture book and have them "read" it to one another.
- Have students write the text or captions for a wordless picture book.
- Send wordless picture books home for families to read in the language(s) they are most rich in.

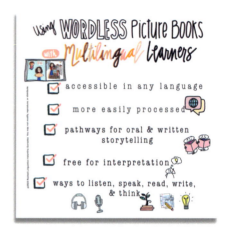

Benefits

- Includes a multimodal learning experience.
- Interactive learning.
- Supports language practice in all domains.
- Offers students a sense of authorship through word choice.
- Accommodates for varied proficiency levels.
- Lowers the affective filter.

INTERACTIVE WORD WALL (IWW)

Interactive Word Walls are word walls with a twist. They are thematic or concept-based rather than random. They are co-created with students rather than teacher-created. Finally, IWWs are graphicly organized rather than alphabetically.

(Jackson, 2013 adapted by Valentina Gonzalez)

Designing Success for Multilingual Learners Second Edition

INTERACTIVE WORD WALL (IWW)

Step-By-Step

1. Examine the grade level state standards and determine what students need to know for the unit of study.
2. Think about the best way for this information to be organized (Venn Diagram, T-Chart, Cycle, Bubble Map, etc.) Draw it out small scale.
3. Plan out critical vocabulary and sentences that align.
4. Create a large-scale, black-line master of the graphic organizer on the wall. Include only the title and subtitles.
5. Invite students to add labeled visuals and real objects to the wall during instruction.
6. Add sentence stems that contribute to the learning at the bottom or sides of the IWW. Model the use of the stems. Then have students practice with partners.
7. Throughout instruction, stop and revisit the IWW to review and model using domain-specific, academic language.

At A Glance

Interactive Word Walls can be used in all content areas and in all grade levels. Because they include visuals and words, they are more accessible to a wider group of learners. IWWs help students link ideas and make connections between words. They are also beneficial for developing oral language skills. As students help to build the IWW, they begin to take ownership of the learning.

Designing Success for Multilingual Learners Second Edition

INTERACTIVE WORD WALL (IWW)

Benefits

- Increases language development.
- Builds academic vocabulary.
- Offers authentic learning experiences.
- Interactive learning.
- Helps make concepts accessible.
- Increases comprehensibility.

Extensions & Modifications

- Invite students to add words in languages other than English too.
- Students can use the IWW as a springboard for writing.
- Take a picture of the IWW and print it small. Have students glue these into their spirals.
- After the unit is complete, the IWW can be taken down and stored on a hanger in the cabinet.

Designing Success for Multilingual Learners Second Edition

SENTENCE PATTERNING CHART (SPC)

The Sentence Patterning Chart helps students practice language structures in a fun, easy way.

Prepare an outline of the chart.

→ Prior to the lesson ←

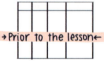

1. Introduce each column ^1 at a time

2. Have students brainstorm words for each column.

(in this order: noun, adjective, verb, adverb (optional), prepositional phrase).

3. List the words students call out. Chorally read each list.

4. Lead students in building sentences. ADJ · NOUN · VERB · ADV · PREP PH

Creative leaders advocate in the classroom.

provides oral language practice   organizes words   opportunity for shared reading & writing

lowers the affective filter   models English language structures   builds vocabulary   engages learners

Designing Success for Multilingual Learners Second Edition

SENTENCE PATTERNING CHART (SPC)

Step-By-Step

1. Create an outline of the chart and present it to the class during a unit of study.
2. Introduce a column at a time and have students brainstorm words.
3. Scribe the words under each column as students dictate.
4. Lead the class in chorally reading all the words when each column is complete.
5. Guide students in creating verbal sentences using the chart.
6. Give students time to practice writing sentences using the chart.
7. Pair students up and have them read their sentences to one another.
8. See the video in the QR code for a way to incorporate song into the sentence patterning chart.

At A Glance

The Sentence Patterning Chart is an authentic method for teaching English language structures while simultaneously teaching content. As the name says, it is a chart that supports sentence patterns or the way words are arranged in a language. The SPC can be implemented in languages other than English too.

SENTENCE PATTERNING CHART (SPC)

Extensions & Modifications

- Use specific colors for each column.
- Pair the SPC with the PWIM.
- Use pictures instead of words or pictures and words.
- Play the Trading Game (see more using the QR code.)

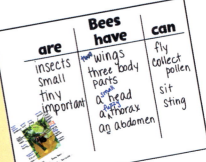

Benefits

- Increases participation.
- Lowers the affective filter.
- Provides an opportunity to practice academic vocabulary.
- Uses repetition to imprint in the brain.
- Strengthens vocabulary.
- Offers an opportunity for shared reading and writing.
- Leverages graphic organization for learning.

Designing Success for Multilingual Learners Second Edition

DEFINE, DESCRIBE, SKETCH

Define, Describe, Sketch is a vocabulary method that uses direct teaching as well as student interaction to enhance vocabulary development.

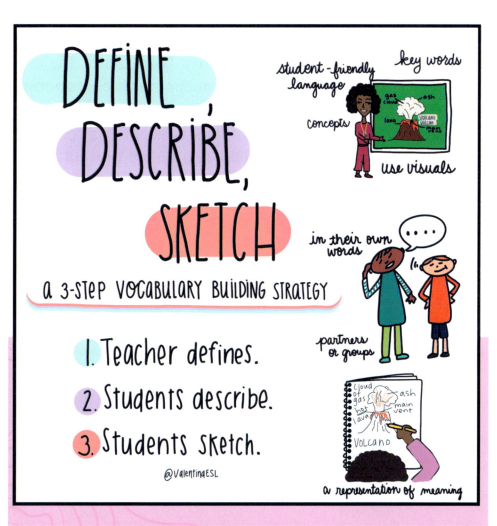

Designing Success for Multilingual Learners Second Edition

DEFINE, DESCRIBE, SKETCH

Step-By-Step

1. Provide students with a clear explanation of a critical vocabulary term or concept using student-friendly language and images, visuals, multimedia, or real objects. Repeat the word often while explaining the definition and have students repeat it with you.
2. Pair or group students and have them share their explanation of the term or concept with one another using their own words. Support multilingual learners with clear expectations and sentence stems for speaking and interacting as you travel around the room listening in to validate and clear up misconceptions.
3. Give students time to sketch a visual representation of the term or concept, reminding them to use words, icons, symbols, and illustrations that help them understand the meaning. Encourage students to express their ideas in the languages they can.

At A Glance

Multilingual learners are building their vocabulary banks in more than one language. Define, Describe, Sketch is a vocabulary-building strategy that incorporates visual notetaking with explicit instruction and peer interaction. This three-step method makes vocabulary learning intentional and personal.

DEFINE, DESCRIBE, SKETCH

Benefits

- Enhances vocabulary development.
- Leverages the power of drawing and visualization.
- Lowers the affective filter.
- Provides an opportunity to practice academic vocabulary.

Extensions & Modifications

- Have student share again using their sketches to explain their definitions one more time.
- Have students meet with a new partner and determine who will be Partner A and B . Partner A defines and describes a vocabulary word and Partner B listens and sketches what they hear. Then the partners switch roles.

Designing Success for Multilingual Learners Second Edition

PARAGRAPH/WRITING RELAY

A cooperative writing technique

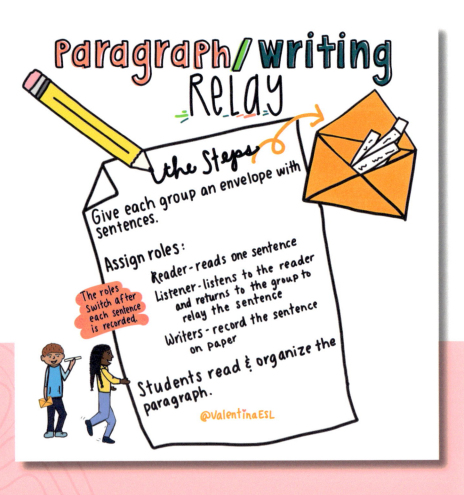

Paragraph/writing Relay

the Steps:

Give each group an envelope with sentences.

Assign roles:

Reader - reads one sentence

Listener - listens to the reader and returns to the group to relay the sentence

Writers - record the sentence on paper

The roles switch after each sentence is recorded.

Students read & organize the paragraph.

@ValentinaESL

PARAGRAPH/WRITING RELAY
A cooperative writing technique

Step-By-Step

Before students arrive:

1. Take a short piece of write such as a paragraph and cut it into sentences.
2. Place the sentences into an envelope.

When students arrive:

1. Group your students. Groups of about four work well. Each group will need an envelope with sentences.
2. Assign each group member roles:
   ○ Reader-reads one sentence from the envelope.
   ○ Listener-listens to the reader and returns to the team to relay the sentence.
   ○ Writers-record the sentence on paper.

*These roles SWITCH after each sentences has been read and recorded.

3. After all of the sentences have been read and recorded, the team works together to reorganize the sentences to make a paragraph.
4. The team reads the paragraph in unison.

Only read one!

Each strip has a sentence on it.

At A Glance

The Paragraph/Writing Relay has students up, moving, and working together to listen, speak, read and write on grade-level text. Students love the game-like, competitive nature of this instructional technique.

A cooperative writing technique

Benefits

- Increases peer interdependence.
- Includes movement.
- Reduces the stress of writing and revising.
- Integrates the language domains: listening, speaking, reading, and writing through peer interaction.

Extensions & Modifications

- Add an additional sentence in the envelope that doesn't belong. After step 3, have students decide which sentences should be removed.
- Have students write an additional sentence to add to the paragraph.
- Instead of four or five sentences in each envelope, envelopes could include words or phrases.
- Visuals could be added to the sentences or replace sentences.

FINISH

44

photo from y-studio

I See-I Think-I Wonder

- What elements of design do you see that make this building accessible?
- What accessibility features do you think are there but you can't see them?
- What do you wonder about the accessibility or the design?
- How what are the connections to lesson design? What are the implications?

Availability is not enough.

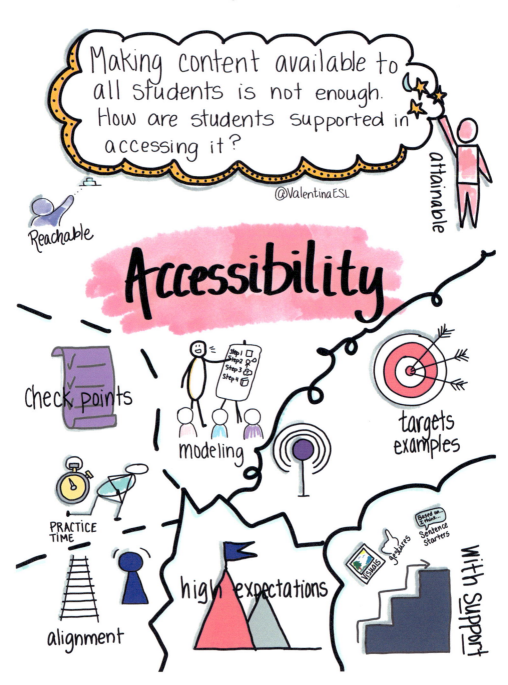

Designing Success for Multilingual Learners Second Edition

Reading Interest Survey

Name:_____

Gonzalez, 2024

Directions: Circle what you love.

sports

animals

mystery

science

cars

nature

fantasy

Reading is fun. ✓ YES ? MAYBE ✗ NO

Circle the one you like best.

Reading alone

Someone reads to me

Reading with friends

Designing Success for Multilingual Learners Second Edition

Reading Interest Survey

Gonzalez, 2024

Name:_____

I get books from _____

My favorite book is_____

I like to read about _____

My favorite place to read is _____

I have books at home.

 Yes

 No

I go to the library:

daily   3 times a week

weekly   never

CLASSROOM LOOK FORS

Classroom Look Fors
Observation checklist.

ROOTED LINGUISTICS LLC.

Objectives	Yes/No/Not Observed	Comments
Content objective is displayed in kid-friendly language.		
Content objective is annotated with synonyms and visuals.		
Language objective is displayed in kid-friendly language.		
Language objective is annotated with synonyms and visuals.		
Learners are referred to the objectives during the lesson and at the closure.		

Grouping	Yes/No/Not Observed	Comments
Learners are intentionally paired and grouped with peers for interaction.		
Learners engage in collaborative practices.		
Learners know the expectations for partner or group interaction.		

Instructional	Yes/No/Not Observed	Comments
Teacher models speaking expectations and complete sentences using sentence stems.		
Sentence stems are available for all learners.		
Learners practice speaking with peers in structured and unstructured methods.		

Imagine schools and classrooms where every student thrives regardless of their language background.
Sound like a dream? It doesn't have to be. Let's join together to make it a reality.
®2023 Rooted Linguistics Valentina Gonzalez. May be photocopied for classroom use.

CLASSROOM LOOK FORS

ROOTED LINGUISTICS LLC.

Material is chunked into smaller more digestible sections.		
Mentor texts and exemplars are available.		
The teacher speaks clearly with an appropriate rate of speech and annunciates.		
Frequent checks for understanding are used as formative assessments.		
The teacher implements wait time allowing for students to process and think.		
The teacher uses gestures to support concept attainment.		
Students are called upon randomly to share responses.		

Material	Yes/No/Not Observed	Comments
Visuals, videos, and manipulatives support concept attainment.		
Learners engage in using English and their other language(s).		
Word banks are available and accessible to learners.		
Graphic organizers and templates facilitate learning.		
Word walls are interactive and visually supported.		
Posters and wall decor are inclusive of all learners.		

ROOTED LINGUISTICS LLC.

Imagine schools and classrooms where every student thrives regardless of their language background.
Sound like a dream? It doesn't have to be. Let's join together to make it a reality.
@2023 Rooted Linguistics Valentina Gonzalez. May be photocopied for classroom use.

Designing Success for Multilingual Learners Second Edition

Listening, Speaking, Reading, & Writing at Home

in the kitchen

Read a recipe

Draw pictures to illustrate the cooking process

Follow a recipe to make a meal
This way

Family Recipes

Write a "how to" book for this recipe

Compare 2 or more recipes

Write a recommendation

Talk about it with a family member, pet, or stuffed animal

with music

Play Karaoke
read

List songs that:
· make you happy
· remind you of someone
· remind you of a time
· make you feel strong
· make you feel . . .

Draw an image to illustrate your favorite song

@ValentinaESL

Compare 2 or more songs

Write a recommendation for a song
- who do you recommend this song for
- why?
- what would you change?

Ask a family member about songs from the past

Listening, Speaking, Reading,& Writing at Home

outdoors

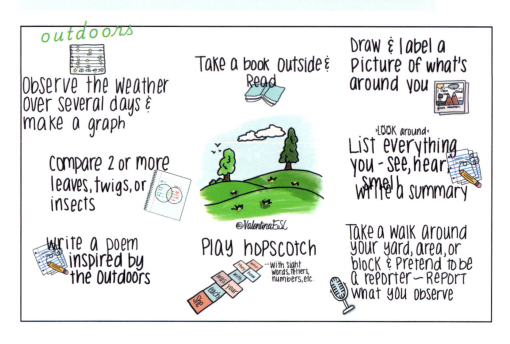

Observe the weather over several days & make a graph

Take a book outside & read

Draw & label a picture of what's around you

Compare 2 or more leaves, twigs, or insects

>LOOK around< List everything you - see, hear, smell write a summary

Write a poem inspired by the outdoors

Play hopscotch --with sight words, letters, numbers, etc.

Take a walk around your yard, area, or block & pretend to be a reporter—report what you observe

@ValentinaESL

with the television

Turn the captions on

Draw pictures to illustrate the main events

Read the captions

List the characters

t.v. Captions ON!
@ValentinaESL

Compare 2 or more characters

Write a summary

Write a recommendation

Talk about it with a family member, pet, or stuffed animal

Notes

Notes

Made in United States
Troutdale, OR
01/24/2025

28294243R00033